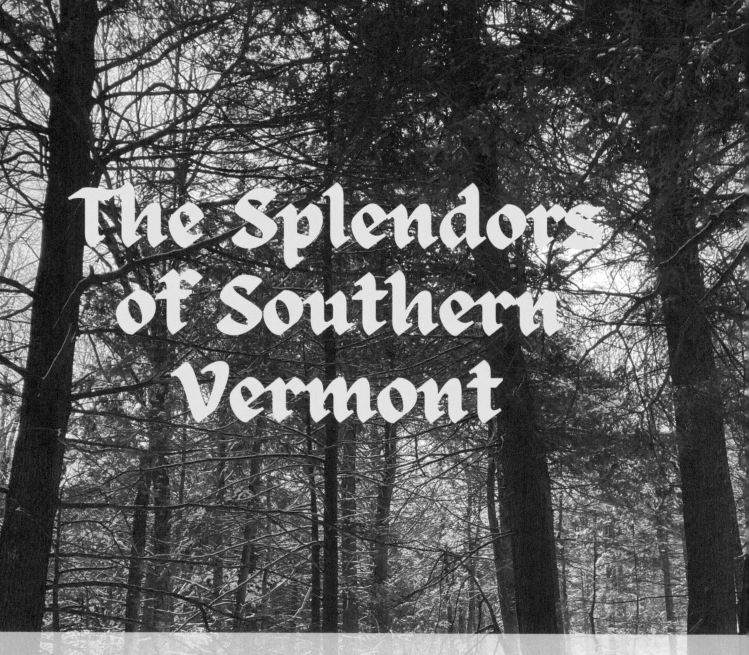

The Splendors of Southern Vermont

A SNAPSHOT IN TIME BY DAN HEALY

Vol. 1

9 781312 508293

Foreward

The photos have all been shot and assembled by the author Dan Healy and feature the surrounding area as it exists in early 2023.

Dan was born and raised in Burlington, the "big city" in the Northwest county of Chittenden Vermont. He graduated from Saint Michael's College only 15 minutes from home and joined the Vermont Air National Guard. After serving a six month deployment in South Korea and Japan, he fell in love with the stark geographic and social contrast of life overseas that didn't quite resemble the suburbia he was used to in Burlington. The farmland and pastures abutting the high rises found in Kunsan and Okinawa drove Dan to look for a life in the city back home. In 2016, he left Vermont for NYC where he met his wife. They relocated to LA for two years while she earned her masters before returning to the TriState area. All the while being away from his home state, Dan realized how good he had it growing up in Vermont. He missed it and wanted to return to the more rural parts of the Green Mountains.

In 2019, the two pounced on the opportunity to purchase a small parcel of land between Mount Snow and Stratton mountain resorts. With the close proximity to two major resorts part of the IKON and Epic pass systems, they understood that skiers and snowboarders from around the world looking to experience what Vermont has to offer would be looking for an affordable place to stay.

In 2021, Dan and his wife Natalie built a small cabin on the parcel and have enjoyed all that it has to offer. They visit frequently, however the cabin is available for short term rentals via AirBnB so they can share the joy it brings with guests from around the world. Many of the photos of the cabin can be found in the pages to follow.

Vermont Foothills

Introduction

This book was created as a photo journal guide to the activities and pleasures Southern Vermont provides, specifically for the traveling guest looking to maximize their experience while staying in the Green Mountains.

Few other places evoke the sense of refreshed vitality as that of the rolling foothills of Southern Vermont. The air is fresh, the mountains are green and the people are warm. This series intends to capture various scenes that can be found around the lower portion of the state, mostly around Route 100, the state highway that functions as the spine of access to some of the best parts of Vermont. Although the biggest industry is tourism and vacationing for enthusiasts of the outdoors, adventure seekers and dairy fanatics, much of the best parts of what the area has to offer is missed by those visiting on long weekends.

The beauty and joy this state has to offer extends far beyond the resorts. Join us as we experience the Green Mountain State in each distinct season starting off with Vol. 1: Spring 2023.

Weekend stays in small cabins such as this provide visitors the oppertunity to fully relish in the sounds, scents and tastes of nature typically associated with camping. With a weatherproof roof and wood stove wor warmth, you get the best of both worlds in a place like this

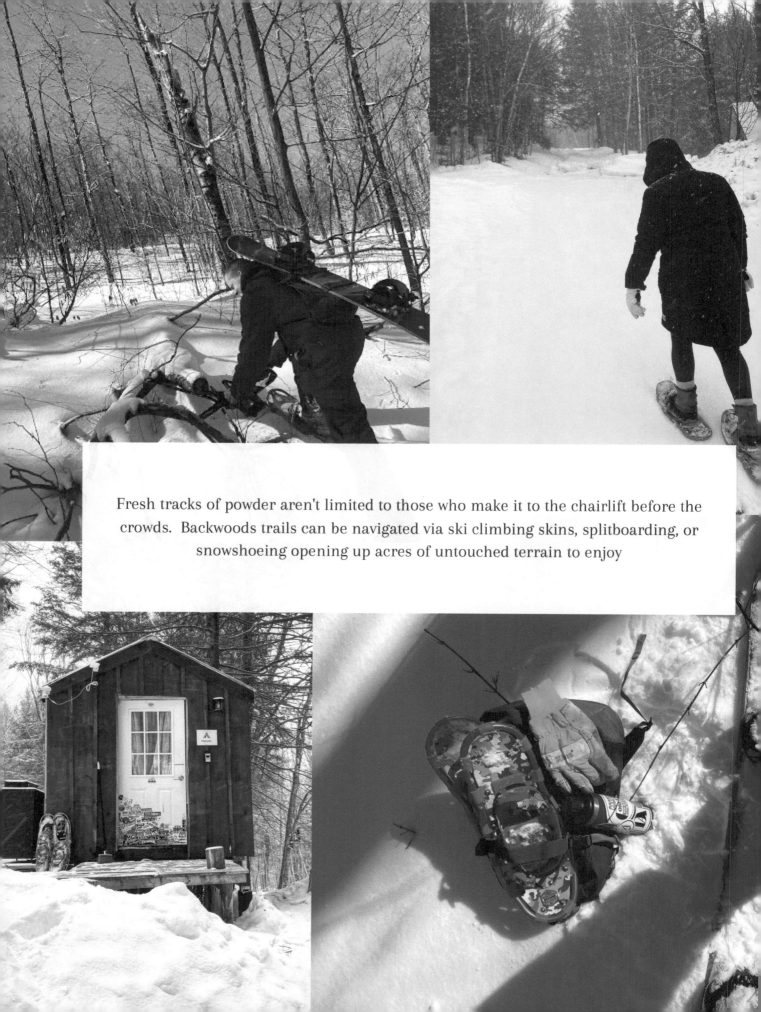

Fresh tracks of powder aren't limited to those who make it to the chairlift before the crowds. Backwoods trails can be navigated via ski climbing skins, splitboarding, or snowshoeing opening up acres of untouched terrain to enjoy

After a modest winter season of variable conditions, Southern Vermont is hit hard with a welcome end of season dumping of snow. The fresh pow helped facilitate the end of skiing season events such as pond skims and the Homesick snowboarding event at Stratton. This event included the likes of pro riders Zeb Powell, Ross Powers and Shaun White celebrating the 90's era of riding with halfpipe, slalom and rail jam events.

Participating riders having a blast getting airborne.
See eaststreetarchives.com for more info on the event

The Green Mountain National Forest is the only public federally managed national forest in the state. The area is protected from development to preserve the habitat and wildlife native to the area. To access and explore the area, most of the forest is only accessible via foot. Ponds such as the one below are otherwise inaccessible. Hiking on designated trails is encouraged and can be found on apps like AllTrails. The most well known trail in the state is The Long Trail, Vermont's portion of the Appalachian Trail extending from the Canadian Boarder down into the Berkshires of Western Massachusetts where it continues down the east coast.

Welcome to the Bourn Pond Moldering Privy

This composting system is maintained by the Green Mountain National Forest and the Green Mountain Club. Proper disposal of human waste is one of our primary concerns in the backcountry. Please help us run this system effectively:

Pee in the woods – this will help keep odors down and will provide the proper moister balance for full decomposition.

Pack out your trash – including food waste, food packaging, paper, and sanitary products.

Toss in a handful of wood shavings after each use – this also keeps odors down and facilitates microbial break down of the waste.

Thank you.

April showers bring May flowers. As a visitor, always
bring waterproof boots and bug spray!

Stratton-Arlington Road cuts through the Green Mountain National Forest connecting travelers from Route 100 to Route 7. This dirt road is unmaintained between November and June making it impassable when it snows, however in the summer months it is a picturesque shortcut to Manchester. Along the road is dispersed camping popular among motorcyclists and overlanders. Spots are available on a first come first serve basis. Expect limited cell service. It's also a great place to bring a head net to keep bugs out of your face

The maple trees are tapped and flowing, the snow has melted as the muddy stick season is the season of harvest for maple sap collectors. The plants sprout and before you know it, the flowers are in bloom and the morning sunlight glows behind the freshly budding green leaves. Put away the ski boots for the season and stock up on bug spray. Spring in Southern Vermont has arrived.

Above: The backside of Stratton visible from a clearing just outside Grout Pond
Below: Ball Mountain Brook along West Jamaica Road

Views from the Ball Mountain Dam

The Ledges is a popular family picnic spot on the eastern shores of the Harriman Reservoir in Wilmington, a hydro power source for much of Western Massachusetts. The area is for day use only, however those looking to cool off can enjoy the lake's serene idyllic landscape from the water. Here, the public is welcome to drop a kayak or paddle board, take a dip, enjoy a BBQ and even venture into the clothing optional area to soak up the sun without worrying about tan lines a safe distance away from the picnickers. This area is lush with friendly wildlife such as frogs, fish, salamanders and other creatures that call the area home. Motor boats and fishing are also authorized, however the boat drop can be found off Route 9, a short 10 minute drive north.

The state of Vermont is full of natural wonder and fun to be had by all.
If you are interested in exploring the area firsthand and found the
cabin photos in this book appealing, consider booking a stay with us at
VTFoothills.com where you will find a link to the AirBnB listing along
with a number of other gifts and keepsakes sourced from the foothills
of the Green Mountain State. Thank you and we hope to see you soon!

Scandia Village
West Wardsboro

VT

VTFoothills.com

Ig: @dirtyalbright

A massive thanks to my wife Natalie for her endless love & support.

Vol 1 - May 2023

CPSIA information can be obtained
at www.ICGtesting.com
Printed in the USA
LVHW010221270623
750892LV00013B/85